A Dangerous Work of Art

And Other Poems

Tej Steiner

A Dangerous Work of Art and Other Poems
by Tej Steiner
© 2021 Tej Steiner
Published by Heart Circle Network, LLC
Ashland, Oregon
www.heartcircle.com

Book design: booksavvystudio.com

ISBN: 978-1-7378934-0-0
First Edition
Printed in the United States of America

*To all the people everywhere
seeking to transform the world
through their personal transformation
and the unleashed creativity and kindness
that follows*

CONTENTS

FROM THE AUTHOR

YOU COULD NEVER CALL ME A PROLIFIC POET. These thirty-one poems have taken me as many years to write.

But there is a reason for this glacial flow.

Rather than being an expression of a sudden insight or an inspirational event, each of these poems captures, instead, my own slow seeding, growth, and flowering awareness of something understood. This awareness-aging process takes time. Lots of time. Even if the writing of the poem itself happens within hours or a day, the necessary gestation happens over time.

These aren't poems so much as they are the worded history of a backyard vegetable garden: planted, cultivated, harvested, and then shared with family and friends.

They are maps with word-pins stuck in them reminding me of where I always am.

They are endless security camera footage where one frozen frame solves the whole damn mystery. Something like that.

Or maybe I'm just a slow poet. Who knows?

I do know that when I read these poems myself over time, I don't tire of them. This could be artistic narcissism, but I don't think so. What it really means is that they aren't mine.

The separated, individual me didn't write them. The more Timeless Me did.

These poems are ultimately about that: the migration of identity from the separated self to the Timeless Self.

Which is a perfect segue to the Timeless You. If you relate to these poems; if they touch you in any way or coincide with your own experience, we will have connected in love, in mutual recognition, even for just a moment.

And isn't that ultimately what all poetry

all art

all love

is about,

Experiencing our shared Oneness?

Tej Steiner

2021

A Dangerous Work of Art

and Other Poems

A DANGEROUS WORK OF ART

From you
A poem is demanded
Or a song from your soul
Or a dangerous work of art.

Do it
Or be damned
To a life as a scribe
In a courtroom empty.

Will your poem
Be fire-filled
Sanitized
Or never consigned to ink?

Will your song
Be sung by one million
By one
Or by no one at all?

Will your art
Be timeless
Praised by liars
Or noticed by no one?

It's your poem
Your song
Your art
Your life
And daily decision.

What will it be?

THE GREAT SURPRISE

Who would have thought
That crawling through this dark, muddy, tunnel
For what seems like lifetimes
Would lead to a magnificent cavern cathedral
A thousand meters high
And vast enough
To hold The Tabernacle Choir
And everything you've always wanted?

Is the caterpillar caught
In The Great Surprise
When it finds it can fly
On satin-colored wings
Made in the dissolution
Of its own body?

Does Spring see itself coming
In the depth of Winter?

Who will you be
And what will you do
When the struggle
You've been in forever
Ends forever?

Love laughs out loud
Seeing our awe and delight
Whenever She shows up
Completely
And totally
Unannounced.

Hold on.
Hold on.

PRESENCE

A lion
Doesn't need to talk about boundaries.
It has teeth.

A redwood tree
Doesn't ask the fern on the ground
What it takes to be rooted.

A hawk
Doesn't have to think about the hunt.
The dinosaurs gave it
Talons
Feathers
Flight
And one hundred and seventy million years
Of focus.

Presence speaks a pure language.
Immutable
Unmovable
It has no need for words
Explanations
Or beliefs.

In presence
Thoughts themselves
Are dust
Just dust
On a grand piano.

WHERE ARE YOU

This is not so much a poem
As it is a personal invitation
To a freedom party
Your own party
Where entry requires
An answer
To an ever-present question.

You can answer this question today
Postpone or decline it
No RSVP is needed.

Where are you right now?

In your house?
In your town?
Your country?
On planet Earth?

No matter what your answer is
Another question will arise.

Where the hell is that?

Sure
Your home is in your neighborhood
Your town is on the coast
Brazil is next to Paraguay
And the Earth is in the Milky Way.

But all these thought-full answers
Get you nowhere.

You can stop this inquiry
And say the question has no answer
Because it just goes on and on.

But does it?

What if you follow the question
Into the night
And as long as it takes
To discover
That you're *here*.

You're *here*.
I'm *here*.

Here is where everyone has the same address.

It's the always *here*
The *here* that has no borders
The *here* we never leave
The nothing outside of *here*
The *here* that holds no time.

As unavoidable as being *here* is
It's easy to think we're somewhere else
Clouds of thought
Memories and emotions
Keep us on the road to getting *here*
Or looking for the imaginary *hereafter*
Instead of simply being *here*.

How far do we have to travel
To get to where we never left?

But being *here*
Must be felt
It's tangible
Discernable
It's alive
It's wonder-filled
It's awareness itself.

Here is known by many names
You can call it what you want
Some name it *Now*
Others *God*
Or *Love*
And some the *All That Is*.

But as a name
I like *here*
A word not confined
To a person
Place
Or thing.

For your freedom party to begin
And never end
This question
Is your invitation to it.

Where are you right now?

Write your answer *here*: _____

HIGH OVERHEAD

Those two red-tailed hawks
Circling high overhead
Floating around and around
With such grace
Seem like they know exactly
What they're doing.

Don't believe this for a moment.

They're actually drunk
Totally drunk on love
Love for each other
In love with Love itself.
They couldn't fly in a straight line
Even if they wanted to.

Rabbits, run free!
Field mice, keep playing!
Scampering squirrels, relax!
They're not hungry for you
They're not even looking down!

Their eyes are locked on one another
Their wings on fire
Their bird-hearts beating wildly.
This is hawk foreplay you're watching.

Actually
Love does this to most birds
It makes them feather-hot
And happy-high.

Once you know
What's really going on up there
You'll see drunk birds
Flying around everywhere.

HE NEVER SAID THAT

Jesus never said
That he was the *only* Son of God.
Who made up that nonsense?
Wasn't him
Maybe Paul
Or a Pope
But not him
They never even met him.

Jesus did say however
After years of seeking
And lonely desert walking
And joyful wonder seeing
That he *was* the Son of God.

Then with light-filled eyes
And that ever-lovin' smile of his
And folded hands in front of his heart
He said quietly
Across the Crease of Time

Life is to discover
Who you really are
I'm with you
I love you

It's your turn now.

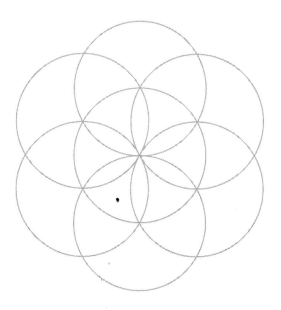

WHICH ONE IS WHICH

Have you ever seen a fly on a horse?
I'm talking about an itsy-bitsy little fly
Perched on the back
Of a big strong horse
Where one's so small
And the other so large?

Just like your Mind
And your Heart
One tiny
And the other vast.

But in you
Which one is which?

Is your Heart the one that's little
While your Mind is bloated with thought?
Or is your Mind the one that's tiny
Compared to your ever-expanding Heart?

Get this ratio right…

And you can fly free

And horse around forever!

NO

That dreaded phone call
From Phoenix, Arizona
At 11:10 in the morning
My daughter's words
Shot through me
Like a poison-tipped arrow
Piercing my heart.

Dad

I don't know how to tell you this

I have cancer.

She died two years later
After doing everything she could
To keep living
While never once complaining
Never finishing her degree
Leaving behind
That closet full of lonely dresses
And a whole community of people
Who loved her dearly.

I'm a father
Who lost his precious daughter.

I have nothing more to say.

WHERE MY LONGING BELONGS

It doesn't get better than this
Finding the stillness beneath my mind
That splashes color
And peace
And sweet music
All over everything.

But why is this journey to stillness so hard?
Why the false turns
The twisted maybes
The bliss one minute
And hell the next?

I just want to stay here
Right here
Right now
Where my longing belongs.

I know that nothing remains the same
That birds don't nest in the North when it's cold
That the East can't hold the sun past noon
That the world keeps spinning away from the West
That the South doesn't get along with Time.

But I don't care about any of that.
I just want to stay here
Right here
Right now
Where my longing belongs.

I want my mind
To fall in love with my heart
Like I did with Mary Lupher
On the first day of Seventh Grade.

I want my endless doubts and questions
To seem as silly to me
As the drunk guy does
Standing in the middle of the street
Half-naked
Confused
Wondering how the hell he got there.

I want all my opinions about everything
To be reversed, cleaned, and cleared
Like my torn T-shirt is
When I take it
From the still warm dryer
Down in the basement.

I just want to stay here
Right here
Right now
Where my longing belongs.

Bats return to their cave at dawn
To sleep upside down in the dark
And quietly smile
At all of us
Who think we know anything
About direction and light.

SOCKS OF FEAR

Take off your dark socks of fear
And wriggle your toes
In wonder again.

Quick!

Before your shoes show up.

MY CRAZY MENTOR

I asked my crazy mentor
What I had to do
To become enlightened.
At first he said
Do nothing
Then with a smile
He said
Do this:

Go way around
The road that's straight

Jog past right
And sprint past wrong

Sit much longer
Than your body can ever stand

And walk across the Arctic snow
Whistling *Way Down South in Dixie.*

Play only games
That have no endings

Sing only songs
That no one remembers

Paint a gorgeous picture
That's three miles long

Catch the falling star
As it shoots across your soul.

Ask your cat to tell you
Everything she knows

Ride the painted stallion
Who answers only to you

Bring home the dog
You've always wanted

Duplicate the pride
In the cougar's eye.

Enjoy yourself
When you think that you are lost

Don't give advice
When your best friend cries

Live like musicians
Whose work is what they play

Tear off the mask
That looks exactly like you.

Wash your lover's body
With rose oil and cream

Make love in the sea
Before the dolphins disappear

Digest the broken glass
That's swallowed in a quarrel

Dance with your partner
Across the floor of Time.

End every war
Before the first shot is fired

Leave behind the prisoners
Who prefer to stay at home

Speak from your wild place
That makes politicians tremble

Bow to the child
Who was never taught to fear.

Entertain a crowd
That's eaten far too much

Build a house by hand
That's mostly made of glass

Swing from a vine
that's anchored to the clouds

Beg a meal from beggars
Then return their bread with gold.

See your world connected
To a thread inside your soul

Wonder where you lost your mind
Then give it no more thought

Know that love's the answer
When the answer can't be found

Know that love's the answer
When the answer can't be found.

WE'RE PRETTY BIG

Sometimes we think
We're pretty small
You know…
Just a grain of sand
On that endless ocean beach…
That small
And insignificant.

But surprise, surprise
The joke's in us
We're not so tiny after all.

As it turns out
Every one of us
Has Everything That Is
Stuffed into us
We're that big!

Everything
I mean every *thing*
Fits snuggly inside of us
Cars, frogs, galaxies,
Horses, houses, rivers,
Governments, socks, and songs,
Tables and chairs,
Highways and history
The sun and the moon
Play yards

Graveyards
And prison yards.

Everything fits into us
Including each other
All with plenty of room to spare.

Who designed this?
And how did it come to be?
What unfathomable brilliance!

But it gets even better!
Whoever it was
Or whatever that is
Is also stuffed into us!

We're the Whole Thing!
Each of us
Equally.

No one has more Everything
Inside of them
Than anybody else.

Why didn't they tell us this sooner?
Years and years
Sitting in those sad and lonely classrooms
And they didn't tell us
That the kids we sat with
That the books we read
And the teachers themselves
Were all inside of us
The whole time!

If we had known this
Think of all the holocausts
We could have avoided.

THE RIDE

Mount me, my Love
My back is strong
Ride me reinless
Holding onto my mane.

Saddle me with your legs
Press your knees to my side
Let the rhythm of my run
And the hardness of my spine
Excite you to fly.

Be relentless in riding
My breathing will hold us
Press me
Claw me
Open my heart
With all your commands.

Drink deeply
Sing loudly
Take all that you deserve
Then more
And then more.

And whenever you're ready
Fly into the sun
Go into it frenzied
As often as you wish
Until the sounds from your throat
Are no longer your own.

Empty everything we are
And everything we aren't
Into Love.

When Oneness has claimed us
And the sun sets slowly
Float me back down
Into a settled walk
Wearing sweat, foam, and tears.
Then…
In stillness
In silence
Dismount
And lie by my side
While I graze
In the sweet green field
Of our light.

MATERNITY WARD

Bunch of babies screaming
In the middle of the night
All lined up in parallel fright
In their pain-glass womb
Away from the breast
They lie alone together
In a motherless nest.

Those bunch of babies screaming
In the middle of the night
Now grown up still in parallel fright
Got to be a man
So acting the part
Making love like crazy
On an empty heart.

Into presidents and dissidents
They each buy a gun
Their women out of earshot
With their tops undone.
Never ending wars
And their no-win scripts
Are the unheard screams
From their empty, soft lips.

Crying out for milk
They milk the land.
Their tiny reach for touch
Becomes a grabbing hand.
Their cry for distant love
Echoes out past the moon
While their marriages end
In frustration-filled doom.

Bunch of babies' futures
All lined up the same
An entire life spent
Thinking they are to blame.
That pain-glass ward
Separating head from the heart
Keeping need and fulfillment
Inch-miles apart.

Senseless separation
At the time of greatest need
The loneliness
Isolation
Planted then as a seed.

Bunch of babies screaming
In the middle of the night
Separated from the others
In their parallel fright.

DOWN TO THIS

After you've done everything you can
After you've searched unsuccessfully
As a bug
As a bird
As a good and bad person
For a way out of the maze
For your ticket to redemption
Doesn't it boil down to this?

You must be willing
To sit in Hell
As long as it takes
To find light
And delight
In the fire.

THE SACRIFICE

Did you ever make potholders
When you were young
Weaving those stretchy-cotton strings
Onto that small, red, metal frame
That had those hooks all around it?

I did
When I was seven.

I remember now
The amazement I felt
Weaving those strands together
Binding them over each other at their ends
Until magically
A potholder emerged
Whole
Complete
Made from any colors I wanted!

I remember wondering
How these bright cotton strings
Could turn into something useful
Beautiful
Like caterpillar becoming a butterfly
But better.

Then came the very best part.
I took my just-made potholder
These strands of cotton
That had sacrificed themselves
To become part of a greater whole
And went to the kitchen
Where my mother was
And I offered it up
To her outstretched hands.

THAT VERY THIN LINE

There's a very thin line
An edge
A narrow pathway

Between accepting
All that is
As Perfect

And choosing
To act
To create
To make things better.

Walk it.

HIGH SCHOOL

I hid my body like a seed
Encased in future tense

My grin was just a decoy
To keep others from my smile

I hid my anger in my pockets
Where I stored my unclenched fists

My tied-up father feelings
Were lacings for my shoes

I wore sadness as a necktie
To say I wasn't so

My raincoat wasn't waterproof
Since my tears were never wet

I held my self-expression in
Like a zipper I'd glued shut

My pants were always way too short
To cover up my urge to please

Just to show how hard I tried
I had my vest grow sleeves

My white shirt lacked sincerity
No wrinkles sweat or stains

I was a mess…

BLIND SERVICE

Don't think you're here
Just to serve others
By doing good deeds
And charity work
While still caught in the duality
Of your own separate self.

Take a closer look now
At the blind crone-lady
You're so gallantly helping
To cross the street.

Don't you see
It's she who's helping you
To cross that street
As you hold onto her arm
With such care?

She's walking you
Through the dangerous traffic
Away from your misperception
That you are separated
From those you serve.

She knows on which side reality resides
And she knows who's serving whom.

Why else would she have tossed you
Her white walking-cane
As she skipped back into the traffic
With such joy?

Take a look at her now
As she patiently waits
For another Good Samaritan
Another soulful person
Who is just as kind
Just as determined
And just as ready as you are
To cross over
Into the Oneness
That you've always
Known was here.

COW AND FROG

Cow standing in the meadow
Unpretentious
Unassuming
Content
Chewing grass
Just grass
Walking slowly
Swatting flies with her tail
With little knowledge
Or care
Of her vulnerability.

Frog sitting still
At the pond's muddy edge
His eyes illuminated
Seeing in the dark
Soaking in simplicity
Unconcerned
That his universe
Is so small
Still
Comfortable
Within his own limitations
And thus
Somehow
Limitless.

Cow and Frog
A lovely couple really
Married in their Beingness
A delight for all of those
Who have the quiet eyes
To see.

I want to be married like this
To merge my vulnerability
With my simplicity
To the point
Where one cannot live
Without the other

Even for a moment.

GOD IS QUITE AN ARTIST

God is quite an artist
He sculpted you and me
Molded all the mountains
Water-colored all the seas.

She painted all the deserts
Pastelled green the grass and trees
God is quite an artist
She sculpted you and me.

He works in rock and bronze and wood
But also flesh and bone
He paints with artist's mastery
Everything that's known.

She shades the newborn baby's skin
With hereditary tone
Fashions stars and galaxies
Giving night a daylight loan.

He weaves a sunset tapestry
For all the world to see
The planet is his gallery
All creatures enter free.

She charcoals black the sky at night
And repaints the world at dawn
She writes a million plays at once
Each play a lifetime long.

God is quite an Artist
He sculpted you and me.

MEMORIAL DAY WEEKEND

Interstate 75
Splitting America down the middle
Like The Mighty Mississippi to the west
Traffic flowing fast and furious
Upstream and down.

It's Memorial Day Weekend
And I'm on the road
To Knoxville, Tennessee
To see my sister and her family.

Painted turtle
Poised on the edge of the highway pavement
Confused
Wondering
What kind of river is this?

The swollen possum up ahead
Cannot answer
Lying stiff
And playing dead forever
A casualty no one will remember
On this Memorial Day in Tennessee.

Sometimes a jet fighter bird
Will buzz my car
While butterflies with hiccups
Play alongside it
Head on, some fat flying insect
Tries to swallow my car whole
Its eyes too big for its stomach
A fatal miscalculation
Splat!

Gracefully
And glaringly
Four turkey vultures
Circle over the highway
Reminding motorists
To watch the thin white line
That separates life from death.

Three small clouds traveling together
In an otherwise perfectly clear blue sky
Perhaps a scouting party
For a storm up ahead.

A defiant old dilapidated barn
Precariously held together
By one remaining rusty nail
Refuses to fall down
Just like the World War vet
Marching in Monday's parade
One rusty medal
Still pinned to his chest
Proudly.

Shamelessly
Off the service road,
A huge old satellite dish
Occupies somebody's tiny front yard
Looking like an ugly exotic flycatcher
Still beaming in 500 channels of distraction
That all buzz around that two-room shack
Making everybody itch
When it's not on.

Highway patrolmen
Paid holiday overtime
Ambush civilian speeders
In an undeclared war
Of cat and mouse
While bales of hay
Once square
Now round,
Watch silently
Ineffectively
Like U.N. observers
From roadside fields afar.

Signs fly by without a heart:
No Trespassing!
No Stopping!
Trust Jesus or Die!

Some signs make me laugh:
Tattoos While You Wait
Wartsberg
Bunnsville
Body Parts Sold Here
Zoom Bait and Batteries.

What's *Zoom Bait?*

The painted turtle
Now a hundred miles back
Still poised at the pavement's edge
Still confused
Wondering
What kind of river is this?

On Memorial Day Weekend
In Tennessee.

INCLUDE EVERYTHING

Leave nothing outside
Your Circle of Delight

Nothing!

Even that insecure boy-president
Who everyday plays
Russian roulette
With his enemies
With our democracy
With the whole world.

Include him.

God does.

Do you have a problem with this?

FEAR NO EVIL

Is it really true
That evil loves to visit
Crowded playgrounds
On cloudy days
To see the children flee in panic
So that it doesn't have to wait in line
For the next available swing?

But what if evil's lonely?
Tired of singing the bully's song
Sick of itself
And being exiled
Into darkness
Where we demand it to be
Out there
Somewhere
Hidden
Unclaimed
Made into something
That our children are taught to fear
And to disown
As something separate from themselves
And way
Way
Way
Too scary to swing beside.

Maybe evil can only smile
When we can smile at evil.

KING IN A CAGE

Talking out loud
And passionately to myself,
My own Lion-Heart
Speaks to my Lion-Mind:

Oh King of the Beasts
Symbol of freedom
Most glorious cat
What are you doing
In this damn zoo?
You don't belong here.

This stinking concrete pen
Where you walk
Back and forth
Day after day
Is no home for any creature
But especially not for you.

Look at you!
A king in a cage
A captive in the commons
Shamefully imprisoned
On display
An object to fill the vacant stares
Of nature-starved people
Who walk their children
Around the zoo
On a leash.

How'd you end up here anyway?
Get caught in thought?
Forget who you were?
Or maybe you figured
It would be fun to be fed
Instead of stalking your own prey.

So what's your game plan
Lion King?

Still talking out loud
And passionately to myself
My Lion-Mind
Answers back
To my Lion-Heart:

Oh
So there you are!
Nice of you to show up
After all these awful years
Which by the way
Have seemed like lifetimes to me.

What could possibly
Have taken you so long to get here?

And how did you think
That I was going to find my way out
Of this particularly dank
Dark and dismal cage
Without you?

You are my Heart
You are my Roar
You are my Power.

It was *you* who disappeared
When I got trapped
Imprisoned in thought
Like everyone else in the forest
As it was cut down
Plundered
And sold.

All of us suffered
All of us casualties of progress
Put in one kind of cage
Or another.

Lion King my ass!
What did you expect me to do
With you
My own heart
Off hiding somewhere
Inaccessible
Spaced out
In another world
All this time?

What *could* I do
But pace back and forth
Back and forth
Back and forth
Until you returned?

I may be a lion
But I couldn't hurry grace.

At the same time
I can't tell you
How great it is
To see you again
To feel my heart
Remember my roar
And experience
The power of my body.

I feel a million times better already.

With you finally back
We can do anything!

Let's get out of here!

THE SOLUTION

How do you get free
From the pain you're in?

I'll tell you how.

Go find a Dragon Slayer
And ask for her sword.

Then
With that blade in hand
Cut all of your fear
Into bite-size pieces
And feed them to your goat.

Goats can eat anything.

ORIGINAL SIN

Instead of being
The Sun itself
I strike a match
And call it Me.

Stone-hearted priests
Mad at the world
And clad in black clothing
Call this *Original Sin*
Then shower us
With shame
And blame
And eternal damnation.

Lighten up
Oh Angry Ones!

This isn't sin
It's just misperception
A blind hand-me-down
From parent to child
That has us all thinking
That we're alone
And separated
From everything else.

Yes
It's the original Missed-Perception.
Instead of being
The Sun itself
I strike a match
And call it Me.

But don't worry
Little Darlin'
It's alright
Just look up

Here comes the Sun!

YOU WILL KNOW

How will you know
That your demons
Have left you?

Well
Crayons will appear
Your crown will open
Your voice will grow mighty
And your feet will take root.

Then
In the terrible mid-day heat
People will gather
Just to sit
And relax
In the sweet
Soulful shade
Of your shadow.

All this
As you color away
In that bright
Bright sunshine
Like there's no tomorrow.

LIKE A CAT BE STILL

Like a cat be still
Until one-pointedness
Directs the pounce.

Patience pays.

Hold the brush high
Until the heart
Moves the hand.

This is art.

Judge not at all
Until the facts
Speak first.

Act only then.

This is all written.

YOUR TIME OF HIDING

We found the crown
You had hidden so well
And we placed it on your head today
Your time of hiding is over.

Those countless years
Spent in the crowded marketplace
Posing as a buyer
Of day-old bread
And spoiled fruit
Have passed
It's time to sit on your throne again.

You have suffered enough
You have died more times
Than you can remember
Your heart is ready to rule.

We're not asking for your opinion about this.

TWO DIFFERENT LOVERS

Like everybody else
You have a choice
Between two very different lovers.

One Lover's name is *Now*.

She has a joyful story
She wants to whisper in your ear
One that requires full focus
Humility
And grace.
It's always a story
You've never heard before.

But you can also choose another lover
Her name is *Time*.

She too will whisper in your ear
But her story is never new
You've heard it
Over
And over
And over
Again.

Time will tell you
That you're young and strong
That you're bold and beautiful
Endlessly special
And in control of everything
Including her.
She's quite convincing.

But then
With no warning at all
She'll just drop you
In a flash
She'll be gone.

You won't know where she went
Or why she left you
You'll feel betrayed
And shaken
Like a dead leaf
Floating down a river
That doesn't care.

You can cry
Scream
Or yell in despair
Punch a hole in the wall
If you want.
Won't matter
Once *Time*'s gone
She's never coming back
She's just like that.

But don't worry
You're not alone
She does this to everybody.

There's a trick here
Of course
It's a simple truth
But sometimes
hard to hear.

Don't mess with *Time*
Treat *Now*
Like she's all there is.

That's it.

Choose to love *Now*
Before *Time* runs out.

TEJ STEINER is the founder of *Heart Circle*, a process used around the world that supports individual transformation though group connection. He is the author of ***Waking Up with Everyone Around Us,*** a pioneering work laying out specific processes through which any social group can create greater trust, transparency, and creativity. He works with individuals, families, community organizations, and businesses while facilitating workshops and online courses in transformational group dynamics. He's also an artist and writer living in Roseburg, Oregon.

www.heartcircle.com

HEART CIRCLE

Also by Tej Steiner:

*Tej Steiner's work is a force of nature, and the
Heart Circle process an evolutionary staple.*

RICHARD GANAWAY, FOUNDER, AO MUSIC

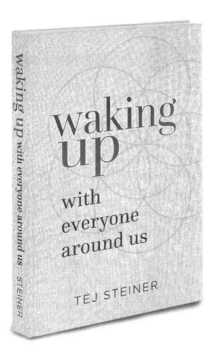

Waking Up with Everyone Around Us—A step-by-step guide, a
book of poetry, a memoir, a life's work all blended together to form
an alive manuscript for how we can support one another in Heart
Awakening and co-creating a Culture of Connection.

Available in softcover, audio, and eBook on Amazon.com
and through all booksellers.
ISBN: 978-0692907092